COLLEGE OUTLINES and OTHER PAPERBOUND BOOKS

published by **Barnes & Noble, Inc.**, 105 Fifth Ave., New York 3, N. Y.

The following paperbound books are intended for both the student and the general reader. The list includes all books in the famous College Outline Series (CO) which summarize important college subjects; many self-teaching books on skills and leisure-time activities; and other significant individual books for adults who wish to broaden their cultural horizons. (These books are available wherever quality paperbacks are sold; the majority of the books are priced at $1.00 to $1.95.)

ART, DRAMA, MUSIC

ART and ANATOMY
ART, HISTORY OF (CO)
MUSIC, HISTORY OF (CO)
MUSIC, INTRODUCTION TO (CO)
OPERA, INTRODUCTION TO
PLAY PRODUCTION (CO)
PLAYS, Plot Outlines of 100
SHAKESPEARE'S PLAYS, Outlines of (CO)

BUSINESS

ACCOUNTING, ELEMENTARY (CO)
ACCOUNTING PROBLEMS (CO)
BOOKKEEPING MADE EASY
BUSINESS ENGLISH
BUSINESS LAW (CO)
BUSINESS MANAGEMENT (CO)
CORPORATION FINANCE (CO)
LAW GUIDE FOR ALL
MARKETING (CO)
MONEY AND BANKING (CO)
SHORTHAND
TYPEWRITING, TOUCH

ECONOMICS

ECONOMIC HISTORY of the
  U. S. (CO)
ECONOMIC THOUGHT, History of (CO)
ECONOMICS, A Dictionary of
ECONOMICS, PRINCIPLES of (CO)
ECONOMISTS PAST and PRESENT
LABOR ECONOMICS and Industrial
  Relations (CO)
STATISTICAL METHODS (CO)
STATISTICIANS, Tables for (CO)

EDUCATION

CHILDREN ASK
EDUCATION, HISTORY OF (CO)
MEMORY, How to Improve Your

ENGLISH

ENGLISH, Common Errors in
ENGLISH GRAMMAR (CO)

ENGLISH (Cont.)

ENGLISH the American Way
GRAMMAR, Rhetoric, & Composition
JOURNALISM, New Survey of (CO)
LETTERS For All Occasions
PUNCTUATION
SPEECH (CO)
SPEECH, Everyday
WRITER'S BOOK

GOVERNMENT

AMERICAN POLITICS, Dictionary of
CONSTITUTION of the United States
GOVERNMENT, American (CO)
POLITICAL SCIENCE (CO)

HANDICRAFTS
HOME IMPROVEMENT

CERAMICS FOR ALL
CONCRETE and MASONRY
DRAW and PAINT, How to
ELECTRICITY in the Home

HISTORY

AMERICAN Colonial & Rev. Hist. (CO)
AMERICAN HISTORY at a Glance
AMERICAN HISTORICAL DOCUMENTS (CO)
ANCIENT HISTORY (CO)
ANCIENT, Medieval, & Modern
  History (CO)
ENGLAND, HISTORY of (CO)
EUROPE, 1500-1848 (CO)
EUROPE since 1815 (CO)
INTERNATIONAL RELATIONS (CO)
MIDDLE AGES, History of (CO)
POLITICAL IDEAS of the American
  Revolution
RUSSIA, History of (CO)
UNITED STATES to 1865 (CO)
UNITED STATES since 1865 (CO)
WESTERN CIVILIZATION, History of
  2 vols. (CO)
WORLD HISTORY at a Glance
WORLD since 1914, History of (CO)

FOLK DANCES FOR ALL

Group dances such as this Danish "Sextur" make it easier to get folks acquainted and to give the dancers a feeling of unity.

EVERYDAY HANDBOOKS

Folk Dances
For All

Collected and Arranged by
MICHAEL HERMAN

Line Drawings by BEN STEIN
Photographs by GJON MILI

BARNES & NOBLE, Inc., New York
Publishers • Booksellers • Since 1873

GV 1743 . H 4

©

Copyright, 1947
By BARNES & NOBLE, INC.

Seventh Printing, 1959
L. C. catalogue card number: 47-11348

All Rights Reserved

Printed in the United States of America

PREFACE

WE call these dances "community folk dances" because that is exactly what they are. These are the dances that are being done by people all over the country in their homes, clubs, churches, schools, parks, and wherever else good folks get together for an evening of fun. Young and old, rich and poor, people of every walk of life, every religion, and every nationality are represented at the usual community folk dance gathering. For folk dancing is fun— folk dancing is easy, and anyone can do it! As one of America's leading recreational activities, it is bringing countless hours of relaxation and pleasure to the American community.

For too long a time folk dancing was an activity associated only with ethnic groups and with folk festivals at which people just sat and watched while others performed. Schools, it is true, did make use of it as a part of their physical education programs; but there the atmosphere was not one of community festivity. Despite the efforts of many individuals and organizations to integrate folk dancing into the American cultural pattern and to adopt it in the community recreational program, it remained more of a special exhibition than something in which to participate.

From 1930 to 1940 various agencies struggled to make folk dancing more of a recreational activity, with the Folk Festival Council of New York doing much of the pioneering in this field. In 1940 impetus to the present-day popularity of folk dancing was given by the New York World's Fair (and coincidentally by the Golden Gate Exposition in California), when thousands of Fair visitors were enticed to try simple dances of many lands at the American Common. Entranced by the fun and by the ease with which they were able to do these dances, these people demanded places in which they could folk dance regularly. There were tennis clubs and bowling clubs—why not folk dance clubs?

901689

Education

To fill this need, the Community Folk Dance Center was set up in New York to service lay folk dancers all over the country. Groups mushroomed in small towns and in sophisticated cities alike. Some were highly organized, others quite informal. All over the country, people discovered that one didn't have to be Swedish to enjoy doing the Hambo, or Russian to enjoy the Troika. By 1945, New York City reported 10,000 registered folk dancers, northern California 5,000; and in between the two states hundreds and hundreds of lay people were folk dancing every night in the week as casually as they would go to the movies. The movement has grown so rapidly that it even boasts a monthly magazine, *The Folk Dancer,* which brings news of groups from coast to coast and acts as a clearing-house for authentic information.

World War II, in place of curtailing folk dance activities, helped to develop them as traveling servicemen spread news of folk dancing both here and abroad. Today, there is more folk dancing going on among lay people than among nationality groups. The Russian gets just as much fun out of doing an Irish dance as the Irishman gets from doing a Russian one. All join hands to share one another's cultural heritage. Folk festival directors now plan for adequate floor space for dancers, rather than for seating accommodations for spectators. The stress is on participation, not on exhibitionism.

Notwithstanding all its fun and gaety, folk dancing brings an even greater contribution to both the participant and the community. Besides "painlessly educating" people in the cultural backgrounds of the countries where the dances originated, it develops good fellowship. Folk dancing is a recognized instrument for breaking down prejudices and for creating in their place a spirit of good will towards all men.

I cannot close without expressing my appreciation to the many ethnic groups in New York City who helped community folk dancing in this country develop as it did and without whose interest and co-operation this book would not have been possible.

MICHAEL HERMAN

INTRODUCTION

IT was no easy task to make selections from the several hundred unpublished folk dances in our collection. Finally it was decided to present a series that, when used together, would form a typical program for a community folk dance gathering and to arrange them in the order which we think best for beginners. The selections include couple, group, round, square, and longway dances, in various tempos, styles, and moods, and represent fifteen different countries. The dances are simple, and most of them can be learned or taught in just a few minutes. This is not to say that they lack color—quite the contrary. They are intensely popular with folk groups all over the nation. Although these selections constitute only a small part of the wealth of folk dances being enjoyed by lay people, they will serve as a basis from which a lively interest can be developed.

There are still many people who have the impression that folk dancing requires special skills, that it demands hours of grueling practice, that one has to sign up for a course in order to learn to enjoy it. A good leader using the dances in this book can disprove this mistaken theory. Even if your group have never danced before— even if they insist that they don't have rhythm or that they cannot tell the right foot from the left—it doesn't matter; for anyone can do the dances in this book. Furthermore, the selections will appeal to advanced folk dancers as well; for despite their simplicity, they are all colorful and gay.

Background notes are given on each dance because without knowledge of the spirit of a dance half the fun is lost. A good leader acquaints his group with this background material. (We use the word "leader" in preference to "teacher," for any formal or pedantic approach to folk dancing will turn people away).

Too much emphasis cannot be put on the fact that folk dancing is fun. That, of course, does not mean that "anything goes." Adherence to authentic forms makes for better folk dancing—but don't worry, this adherence does not in any way detract from the fun.

One of the problems facing the folk dance movement today is the temptation to emphasize exhibitions. Frankly, the folk dance was never meant to be watched (as many a spectator can substantiate after watching what seem to him to be the same patterns and steps over and over again). Aware of this lack of theatrical appeal, some folk dancers try to dress up the dances, or they seek out difficult ones which require special skills and long hours of practice. The result is that the original purpose behind folk dancing is lost in the desire to attract an audience. The gist of this problem was very adequately stated in a column by John Martin, dance editor of the *New York Times,* when he said: "As soon as the dancer ceases to dance for his own pleasure and begins to consider what the spectator thinks of his performance, he departs from the original spirit of the thing he is doing and changes its essential character." Need we say more?

Our artist, Ben Stein, has made sketches for this book, not to be ornamental (although we think they are that, too), but to illustrate each step clearly and precisely. Gjon Mili's high-speed photographs of folk dancers in costume give additional spice to the book. The pictures are not in every instance specifically related to the dances with which they appear, but they impart some of the spirit of folk dancing that is impossible to the printed word.

With all this in mind, if you still have any doubts about your ability to go folk dancing, take a look at page 30, where you will see a photograph of rotund, famed ballad-singer Burl Ives, weight 300 pounds, who can and does go folk dancing for three hours at a stretch without any qualms. What's to keep you from it? Let's go folk dancing!

TABLE OF CONTENTS

xi

PRONUNCIATION KEY
AND RECORD GUIDE

Pronunciation of Dances	*Recommended Records**
Danza — Dahn' za	Folk Dancer MH 1045
Eide Ratas — I-deh Rah' tahs	Folk Dancer MH 1018
Kohanochka — Ko-ha' noch-kay	Folk Dancer MH 1058 or K 101
Kreuz Koenig — Kroytz Koy' nikh	Folk Dancer MH 1022
Kujawiak — Koo-ya' vyak	Folk Dancer MH 1019
Landler — Land' ler	Victor 25-4097
Mexican Waltz	Folk Dancer MH 1016
Norwegian Polka	Folk Dancer MH 2001
Ohorodnik — O-haw-rud' nik	Folk Dancer MH 1066
Patch Tanz — Pahtch Tahnz	Folk Dancer MH 1092
Red River Valley	Folk Dancer MH 3013
Sextur — Sex' toor	Folk Dancer MH 1021
Tarantella	Victor 25-7061
To Ting — Toe-ting	Folk Dancer MH 1018
Trip to Helsinki	Methodist 106
Troika — Troy' ka	Folk Dancer MH 1059 or K 104
Tropanka — Tro-pahn' kah	Folk Dancer MH 1020
Varsovienne — Var-so-vee-enn'	Folk Dancer MH 1023
Weggis — Ve' kiss	Folk Dancer MH 1046

*Distributed by *The Folk Dancer*. P. O. Box 201, Flushing, New York

THE
BULGARIAN TROPANKA

W E are going to assume that you have before you a group of people who have never folk danced before. By using the dances in the order presented in this book and by following the suggested techniques, you will be able to lead the group smoothly and easily from the very simple to the more complicated dances. Ready to begin?

The first problem is to get the people onto the floor. You must anticipate a certain amount of reluctance — some will be shy, others boisterous. Therefore, the first dance must be wisely chosen to counteract these attitudes. The Bulgarian Tropanka is ideal for this purpose. It requires no partners — obviating the problem of "coupling up" the group. You entice the people into a single circle with hands joined, using such calls as: *Everybody up on the floor! No partners needed! Anyone can do this dance! It's just for fun! All you do is run, stamp, and shout!*

Now stand in the middle of the circle and proceed to show how easy it is to do the Tropanka by demonstrating just the first part — the running to the right and to the left with the stamp. Ask everyone to imitate you, as you do it once more in the center so that all can see you. There, that was easy, and by this time the heavy stamping has broken down any atmosphere of shyness that may have hovered over the crowd.

Before you proceed to show the rest of the dance, explain that the purpose in stamping the foot is by no means to look graceful: the toe should be turned out in a somewhat awkward manner

1

(see Diagram 2). This little quirk makes for good Bulgarian style and, needless to say, makes the dance so much more fun to do. At the beginning there is bound to be a considerable amount of bungling and awkwardness in the group: the awkward steps of this dance will prevent the people from being too aware of their own lack of grace and will add to their confidence. Now go ahead and teach each part of the dance as in the directions.

The dance should not be done more than three times. That is enough to show the group that they can do it, and it will not leave them too tired for the next dance. Be sure not to forget the hearty shout in the third figure.

This dance was introduced to the Community Folk Dance Center of New York by Dimitri Colchagoff of Ohio.

You'll find plenty of humor in folk dances. In this Swedish dance the man falls for the lady both literally and figuratively. Note the wooden shoes.

TROPANKA

THE DANCE

Bulgarian Stamping Dance

Formation: For as many couples as will—in a single circle, all hands joined. Partners are not necessary. (See Diagram 1.)

Music: Count "one—and—two—and" to each measure.

First Figure

Diag. 1

Meas. 1-2: Beginning with the right foot, all take five running steps to the right (right—left—right—left—right; *counts "one—and—two—and—one"*). Cross left foot over right foot and stamp twice in place with the left (*counts "and—two"*). See Diagram 2 for the stamp. Pause (*count "and"*).

Meas. 3-4: All turn to the left and take five running steps forward (clockwise), beginning with the left foot. Cross right foot over left and stamp twice.

Diag. 2

Meas. 1-4 (repeated): Repeat above action.

Second Figure

Meas. 5: All face the center of the circle and step on the right foot to the right side (*count "one"*). Hop on the right foot, at the same time swinging the left in front of the right (*count "and"*). Step on the left foot to the left side (*count "two"*). Hop on the left foot, swinging the right in front of the left (*count "and"*). (See Diagram 3.)

Diag. 3

Meas. 6: Step on the right foot to the side (*count "one"*). Cross left foot over right and stamp twice with the left (*counts "and—two"*). (See Diagram 2.) Pause (*count "and"*).

Meas. 7-8: Same as Measures 5 and 6 in reverse. All begin with the left foot.

Third Figure

Meas. 5-8 (repeated):

Meas. 5: All step forward toward the center of the circle with the right foot (*count "one"*). Hop on the right foot (*count "and"*). Step forward with the left foot (*count "two"*). Hop on the left foot (*count "and"*). Dancers move toward the center of the circle with a loud shout of "Hey!" and gradually bring hands up, finishing as in Diagram 4.

Diag. 4

Meas. 6: Step forward with the right foot (*count "one"*). Stamp twice in place with the left foot (do not cross over; *counts "and— two"*). Pause (*count "and"*). (See Diagram 4.)

Meas. 7-8: Repeat Measures 5-6 dancing backward to original places, beginning with the left foot and gradually lowering hands.

Meas. 9-16: As in Measures 1-8.

The Danes are great lovers of the quadrille form of dance. Many American square dance figures have their roots in Scandinavian dances like this one.

THE
RUSSIAN TROIKA

NOW we are ready for the second dance. The group is more confident, but as yet not confident enough to couple off. The Russian Troika will break up the circle into more intimate sets of three people and still give a group feeling. Actually, it is a good dance to use as a "beginner," but, in general, not so good a choice as the Tropanka since it requires the formation of sets.

Although the dance was originally done with one man and two women, it is permissible to make adjustments to fit the needs of the gathering. Thus it can be done with one woman and two men, with three women, or with three men. Do the dance through with the group once or twice before you make it progressive — but progressive it should be, as in this manner dancers become acquainted with each other without the necessity of formal introductions.

The glamour of Russian dances has made them universally popular; and, contrary to general opinion, they are not all difficult to do. The Troika, using only a simple running step set to lively music, retains all the Russian flavor.

When the record for this dance is played, you may be wise in lifting the needle before the end — as it may be too long and tiring for the average group. When the dance is used, as it often is, for the concluding number of a set of dances, however, let the record run its full course. The people will be tired, but delightfully so.

TROIKA

THE DANCE

Russian Dance

Diag. 1

Formation: Groups of three around the room — all facing counterclockwise. Traditionally, the center person of each group should be a man — the other two, women. The center person joins hands with each of the others. Free hands are held on the hips. (See Diagram 1.)

Music: Count "one—and—two—and" to each measure.

First Figure

Meas. 1: Four running steps diagonally forward to the right, all starting with the right foot.

Meas. 2: Repeat diagonally forward to the left.

Meas. 3-4: Eight running steps directly forward (counterclockwise), beginning with the right foot.

Meas. 5-6: Keeping her hands joined with his, the woman on the man's right runs in front of him, under an arch formed by him and the left-hand woman, and back to place with eight running steps. The other two run in place, with the man turning to the left under his own left arm as the right-hand woman runs underneath the arch. (See Diagram 2.)

Diag. 2

Meas. 7-8: The woman on the left runs under an arch formed by the man and the right-hand woman and back to place with eight running steps.

Second Figure

Meas. 9-11: Each group of three joins hands in a single circle and runs to the left (counterclockwise) with twelve running steps, beginning with the left foot. (See Diagram 3.)

Meas. 12: Three stamps in place (left—right—left; counts *"one—and—two"*). Pause (*count "and"*).

Meas. 13-16: Keep hands joined and run to the right (counterclockwise) with twelve running steps; finish with three steps in place. Women release hands and all continue to dance with the same partners.

Diag. 3

To make the dance progressive, in Measures 13-16 of the Second Figure all dance to the right with twelve running steps. The man at the twelfth step should be facing line of direction (counterclockwise). Continue with four more running steps, the man running under joined hands of the women and releasing their hands. He continues forward to join the next group ahead, while the women dance in place.

Lowicz costumes from Poland enhance the chorus figure of the "Kujawiak," described on page 80.

THE
JEWISH PATCH TANZ

YOUR group by now is pretty well winded; so it's time for a slow and easy dance. Be sure to announce that it is going to be slow and easy, lest some of the members want to sit down and rest. Ideal for just such a moment in the program is the Jewish wedding dance the Patch Tanz (sometimes called "Clap Dance"). It, too, is progressive, providing opportunity for an exchange of partners.

As partners are necessary in the Patch Tanz, the leader must couple off the circle, making sure that each man has a woman on his right-hand side. Ask the couples to face each other for a moment and say "Hello" so that they will know they are partners. Since the dance is so simple, it depends wholly on its style to give it charm. Observe carefully, therefore, the directions given for the use of the strut step (instead of a mere walk), for the position of hands, etc.

Teach each part separately. The first time through, stop and say to the circle, "Every man should have a new lady on his right-hand side — if not, someone doesn't want to share his partner." This will save those who have failed to execute the figure properly from feeling embarrassed or conspicuous. Allow time for the correction to be made and start the dance over again.

After all have learned the dance, add the introduction as follows: before the dance begins, all rise up on their toes and come down on their heels four times to the four chords of introduction in the music. The last time the dance is done, the leader shouts, "All join hands quickly"; and the dance is finished with the

circle raising joined hands sharply up, down, and up to the three
final chords. The leisurely tempo and the constant change of
partners make this one of those dances that can be done for a
longer spell than others. Be sure to retain a gay spirit throughout
the dance, reminding the dancers that they should imagine themselves at a wedding all having a fine time.

Lillian Shapiro first taught this dance at the New School for
Social Research.

Aino Vare's Finnish group demonstrates a position found in many folk
dances; it is usually called a "swing your partner." Note the similarity between this photo and the one of the same figure, American style, on page 74.

PATCH TANZ

THE DANCE

Jewish Wedding Dance

Formation: As many couples as will—in a single circle with joined hands bent at the elbow and held at shoulder level. (See Diagram 1.)

Music: Count "one—and—two—and" to each measure.

Diag. 1

Step: A walking step throughout the dance done as follows: Step forward to the right on the right foot (*count "one"*); bend the right knee (*count "and"*); step forward with left foot (*count "two"*); bend the left knee (*count "and"*). In circling to the right turn the body in the direction you are going.

First Figure

Diag. 2

Meas. 1-4: All circle to the right (counterclockwise) with eight walking steps. Begin with the right foot. See description above under "Step." (See Diagram 2.)

Meas. 5-8: All circle to the left beginning with the right foot.

Second Figure

Meas. 9: All dancers take two walking steps forward towards the center of the circle, beginning with the right foot.

Meas. 10: All clap their own hands three times (*counts "one—and —two"*). Pause (*count "and"*).

Meas. 11: All join hands and take two steps backwards away from the center—back to original places (men begin with the left foot, women with the right foot). As they reach their places, all drop hands and face partners.

Meas. 12: All stamp three times in place, using the heel (man stamps left heel; woman her right).

Meas. 13: All join hands again and walk toward the center with two walking steps.

Meas. 14: Repeat Measure 10.

Meas. 15: Repeat Measure 11.

Meas. 16: Repeat Measure 12.

Diag. 3

Third Figure

Meas. 17-20: Partners join opposite hands (woman's left in man's right, and her right in his left; see Diagram 3). The man keeping his partner on the right, with arms outstretched at shoulder level, the couples walk forward with eight steps turning (clockwise) in place.

Meas. 20-21: The men change places with partners on the left and walk in the opposite direction (counterclockwise), continuing to walk throughout Measures 23 and 24. Four walking steps.

Meas. 23-24: Partners keep inside hands joined (man's left, woman's right) and raise joined hands overhead. Outside hands are released. Under raised arms, the woman walks in front of the man over to the man's left and remains there. Four walking steps. (See Diagram 4.)

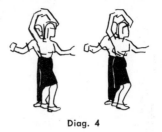

Diag. 4

All join hands again and do the dance all over with new partners on the men's right. Special attention should be given to see that each dancer uses the strut step rather than a plain walking step. The strut adds style and color to the dance, gives it distinctive character, and makes it more fun to do.

Full skirts are a must in folk dancing. They are comfortable and make a pretty pattern when the women twirl. In this Polish dance, men bend low to catch a glimpse of the ruffled petticoats below.

THE
MEXICAN WALTZ

AT last we are ready for a couple dance. Although called the "Mexican Waltz" and done to the Mexican tune *Chiapanecas,* this is *not* a Mexican dance. That point should be made clear when teaching the dance, lest it be confused with the authentic Mexican dance Chiapanecas. It is an American dance popular in the southwestern part of the United States. Al MacLeod of the Freeport Country Dancers in New York introduced it and made it popular in the East.

To make it more interesting to the group, you might report that Gene Kelly used this dance in his picture *Anchors A-weigh* and that he learned it while folk dancing in New York.

MEXICAN WALTZ

Sprightly waltz

THE DANCE

American Couple Dance

Formation: A dance for as many as will—in a double circle around the room: men on the inside, their partners on the outside. All join inside hands (man's right, woman's left) and place free outside hands on hips. All face counterclockwise in circle. (See Diagram 1.)

Diag. 1

First Figure

Meas. 1: Partners step on the outside foot (man's left and woman's right) for *count "one."* Swing free inside foot across and in front of outside foot for *counts "two—three."* (See Diagram 1.)

Meas. 2: All step (stamp) in place on the inside foot (man's right, woman's left) for *count "one."* Swing outside foot in front and across the inside leg.

Meas. 3-4: Place outside foot down beside inside foot with a slight stamp (*count "one"*). Pause (*count "two"*). Partners release hands and clap their own hands twice (*counts "three—one"*). Pause (*counts "two—three"*).

Meas. 5: Partners turn about in place to face the opposite direction (clockwise). They join inside hands again (man's left, woman's right). Repeat Measure 1 by stepping on the outside foot (man's right, woman's left) and swinging inside foot across.

Meas. 6-8: Same as in Measures 2-4, using opposite feet.

Second Figure

Meas. 9: Partners face each other and join both hands (right with partner's left and left with partner's right). Partners balance by stepping backward on the left foot (*count "one"*; see Diagram 2). Pause for *counts "two— three."*

Meas. 10: Partners step forward toward each other on the right foot (*count "one"*). Pause (*counts "two—three"*). At the same time their arms are stretched out to the side at shoulder level. (See Diagram 3.)

Diag. 2

Meas. 11-12: All step back on left foot (*count "one"*) and release hands. Pause (*count "two"*). Partners clap their own hands twice (*counts "three—one"*). Pause (*counts "two —three"*).

Third Figure

Meas. 13: Join hands as in Diagram 2 and step forward in a balance on the right foot (*count "one"*). Pause (*counts "two—three"*). Arms are outstretched at shoulder level as in Diagram 3.

Diag. 3

Meas. 14: Step backward on the left foot (*count "one"*). Pause (*counts "two—three"*).

Meas. 15-16: Step forward on the right foot, release joined hands (*count "one"*). Pause (*count "two"*). Embrace partner and clap own hands behind partner's back (*counts "three—one"*). Pause (*counts "two—three"*). (See Diagram 4.)

Diag. 4

Fourth Figure

Meas. 17-32: Couples in ordinary dance position waltz around the room with sixteen waltz steps.
Repeat as many times as desired.

This dance can also be done in square formation. Start the dance by having all join hands and waltz to the left and then to the right (Measures 17-32). Partners then do the dance from the beginning (Measures 1-16). Now they turn to their corners and waltz around the set. The dance is repeated until all are back with their original partners.

THE
DANISH SEXTUR
(Six Dance)

THE Danish Sextur has been called the "perfect folk dance" because it is simple, has a moderate tempo, has enough figures to make it interesting, has music that is melodious, and is a group dance requiring the co-operation of all twelve partners in the set. Many of the figures resemble those found in American square dances, and the dance is often referred to as a "six-couple square dance."

After your circles, of six couples each, are formed, have the couples number themselves off from one to six and ask Couples One and Four, Two and Five, and Three and Six to raise their hands in turn so that they will know with whom they are to dance across the set. Teach the chorus of the dance before you show the figures, since the figures are simple enough. Sometimes it is a good idea to substitute a simple walking step instead of the chassé in the chorus until the group has mastered the chorus figure — and then to demonstrate and teach the chassé step as the authentic way of doing the dance.

In the "Grand Right and Left" figure, the hands are extended at shoulder level (as customary in Scandinavian dances) rather than at waist level. In the last figure, care should be taken that couples face each other directly and pivot in place in time to the music. There is a tendency to do this figure as one would a buzz-step turn in a square dance, the partners standing with right shoulders touching and buzz stepping around; this should be avoided.

20

Warn the group that Couples One and Four must be ready to start the chorus after each figure, so that they won't take too long a time in getting back to place. Usually done once through, the dance is so popular that it is often done twice. The Sextur is here given as done by the Danish Folk Dance Society, Carl Hansen leader.

Red or black boots are characteristic of Slav costumes. They are the favorite footgear of lay folk dancers, too. Kazimiera Brytczuk here wears a Polish costume of Krakow.

SEXTUR

CHORUS

Fine

Grand Right and Left

4 times DC al Fine

THE DANCE

Danish Group Dance

Formation: Six couples—in circle with hands joined. Couples are numbered from one to six, Couple One standing with back toward the music.

First Figure

Meas. 1-8: All dance sideward to the left with sixteen slides back to place.

Chorus

Meas. 9-10: Couples One and Four (with inside hands joined and outside hands on hips) dance forward toward each other with one chassé step and two ordinary walking steps (see Diagram 1) as follows:

Diag. 1

MAN'S STEP: Beginning with left foot (outside foot), move forward one step (*count "one"*), bring the right foot up (*count "and"*), and step forward on the left (*count "two"*). Pause (*count "and"*). Take two ordinary walking steps forward with the right (*count "one"*) and then the left (*count "two"*) foot.

WOMAN'S STEP: Same as the man's but with opposite feet.

Meas. 11-12: Couples Two and Five dance forward in the same manner with the outside foot. At the same time, Couples One and Four dance back to place beginning with the inside foot (man's right, woman's left).

Meas. 13-14: Couples Three and Six dance forward toward each other while Couples Two and Five dance back to place in the circle.

Meas. 15-16: Couples Three and Six dance back to place in the circle in time for the "right and left" which follows.

Diag. 2

Meas. 17-24: "Grand Right and Left." Partners face each other, give right hands and pass each other by the right shoulder, give left hands to the next dancers and pass on the left shoulder—and continue in this manner all the way around the circle and back to their original places. (See Diagram 2.)

Second Figure

Meas. 1-8: Men stand in place clapping hands while the women join hands in the center of the circle and slide to the left ONCE around with sixteen steps, returning to their partners in time for the chorus. (See Diagram 3.)

Meas. 9-24: Chorus.

Meas. 17-24 (repeated): As before.

Diag. 3

Third Figure

Diag. 4

Meas. 1-8: Women stand in place while the men join hands in the center of the circle and slide to the left TWICE around with sixteen steps, returning to their original positions beside partners. (See Diagram 4.)

Meas. 9-24: Chorus.

Meas. 17-24 (repeated): As before.

Fourth Figure

Meas. 1-8: Partners take shoulder-waist position (the man holds the woman around the waist and she places both hands on his shoulders) and couples turn in place with a walking step. Partners face each other throughout the turn. (See Diagram 5.)

Meas. 9-24: Chorus.

Meas. 17-24 (repeated): As before.

Diag. 5

Finale

Meas. 1-8: All join hands in one circle and slide to the left with sixteen steps.

You've got to have lots of pretty petticoats for this woman-tossing figure with which many a folk dance is finished off. Although this seems to be hard work for the man, it is actually the woman who leaps in the air and gives the spectator the impression that her partner is a man of great physical prowess. For a reverse situation, see the photo on page 36.

This is a good example of the humorous touches found in folk dances. It is one of the figures of the Swedish "Oxdans." Designed for men only, the Oxdans is often used when there is a predominantly male gathering.

THE
NORWEGIAN POLKA

THERE are as many variations of the polka as there are countries on this earth. There are the Polish Polka, the Heel-and-Toe Polka, the Finger Polka, the Butterfly Polka, the Polka Koketka, etc.—all of them of a vigorous nature. The Norwegian Polka is the only one that does not use the polka step. Perhaps that's what makes it so easy to do and, as a result, so popular. Its simple walking step and pivot require no unusual output of energy.

You can dance the Norwegian Polka to almost any kind of polka music, but discerning folk dancers learn to recognize the difference between music for the polka—Norwegian style—and music for the polka—other styles. The Norwegian Polka music has more of a march tempo and is always played in intervals of eight measures.

As in all Scandinavian dances, it is important to keep the free hand on the hip. Besides being authentic, this gives you a good appearance.

Folk dancers usually don't tolerate any intermissions at their gatherings. Instead of sitting, they rest up by doing a Waltz, Schottische, Hambo, or Polka. The Norwegian Polka is an ideal "intermission dance." Folks like to do it several times during a session, each time to a different melody. No specific record is really recommended, since there are many good Scandinavian Polka records available. The dance was introduced by Aasmund Goytil, leader of the Norwegian Folk Dance Group of New York.

NORWEGIAN POLKA

Tempo di polka ♩ = 114

THE DANCE

Norwegian Couple Dance

Formation: For any number of couples—a double circle around the room, men in the inside circle, their partners in the outer circle. All face counterclockwise with inside hands joined (man's right, woman's left). Outside hands on hips.

First Figure

Meas. 1-2: Beginning with the outside foot (man's left, woman's right) all take three walking steps forward (*counts "one—two—one"*). Swing inside foot forward and upward at the same time, lifting the heel of the outside foot (*count "two"*). Do not hop. (See Diagram 1.)

Diag. 1   Diag. 2   Diag. 3

Meas. 3-4: Change hands and walk forward in the opposite direction (clockwise) in the same manner. Man begins with the right foot, his partner with the left. (See Diagram 2.)

Second Figure

Meas. 5-6: Change hands and face counterclockwise again, walking forward with four steps beginning with the outside foot (man's left, woman's right). Turn toward partner on the last step.

Meas. 7-8: Take partner in ordinary dance position (see Diagram 3), and turn with partner clockwise, counterclockwise around the circle with four walking steps or pivot.

Repeat the same for every eight measures.

Two of the most common figures found in folk dances are the open position and the schottische step, illustrated here by Burl Ives, in American farmer costume, and his partner, in Polish costume.

THE
SWEDISH VARSOVIENNE

THE dances given so far have required no complicated steps. Now is the time to introduce a dance requiring more thought. Remember that not everyone in the group is going to learn it thoroughly at the first session. The idea now is to give a general picture of it, relying upon repetition at future sessions to bring perfection.

Before teaching the dance, it is well to acquaint yourself with some background material about it. There has been much controversy concerning its origin. Claims that it is a Polish dance are based upon the contention that the name *Varsovienne* means "Warsaw"; but, even if so, this means little. The dance has never been a part of Poland's dance culture, and the habit of naming dances after big cities, prominent people, etc., has been prevalent in many countries. (The "French Reel" and "Paris Polka," for instance, are not French, nor is "Old Berlin" German—all three are Danish.) The Varsovienne may equally well have been Swedish, French, Italian, Spanish, or Mexican American — for various forms (under various names and spellings) have been found in many different countries. In our own United States, Texas has a popular version called "Put Your Little Foot." Colorado, California, and New Mexico have a different version called "La Varsovianna."

The Varsovienne in this book is a Swedish dance, done only to the music which is provided for it. Both ballroom and peasant renditions are given. One reason that the Swedish Varsovienne is so popular is that the waltz interlude, lacking in other versions, prevents monotony.

In teaching the dance, make sure that the dancers use the heel and not the toe where so directed. (The toe is used in "Put Your Little Foot," and that is why American dancers sometimes tend to use toe instead of heel.) Free hands, as in all Scandinavian dances, are kept on hips. It will help if the leader calls out the steps for the second figure as: "one-two-hop; one-two-hop; one-two-three; heel-two-three," etc.

The Swedish Folk Dance Society of New York introduced the Varsovienne to folk dancers in that city with Sture Lilja as leader.

VARSOVIENNE

THE DANCE

BALLROOM VERSION

Swedish Couple Dance

Formation: For as many couples as will—in a double circle around the room. Men on the inside, women on the outside. All face counterclockwise.

Position: Woman is on the man's right. The man's arm is extended behind (across) his partner's shoulders so that his right hand holds her raised right hand. Her left arm is stretched out in front of the man's chest and her left hand rests in his left hand. (See Diagrams 1 and 2 and photograph on page 50.)

First Figure, Music A

Meas. 1: Partners change places by taking three walking steps beginning with the left foot. The man moves to his right passing behind his partner (L—R—L); the woman moves to her left and in front of man (L—R—L). (*Counts "one*

Diag. 1

—two—three.") Man is now on the outside with his partner on his left as in Diagram 1.

Meas. 2: Extend right foot forward and slightly to the right and place right heel to the floor, toes up (*count "one"*). Hold for *counts "two—three."*

Meas. 3: Partners change back to original places by taking three steps, both beginning with the right foot. Man moves to his left passing behind partner (R—L—R) while woman moves to her right passing in front of the man (*counts "one—two—three"*).

Meas. 4: Place left heel to floor, toes raised (*count "one"*). Hold (*counts "two—three"*). (See Diagram 2.)

Meas. 5-8: Repeat Measures 1-4.

Second Figure, Music B

Meas. 9: Beginning with left foot, partners dance forward with two walking steps (*counts "one—two"*). Hop on the right foot (*count "three"*) lifting left foot.

Meas. 10: Repeat Measure 9.

Diag. 2

Meas. 11-12: Repeat measures 1 and 2 (changing places).

Meas. 13: Man is now on his partner's right as in Diagram 1. Partners take two walking steps forward beginning with the right foot (R—L; *counts "one—two"*). Hop on the left foot, lifting right foot (*count "three"*). (See Diagram 3.)

Meas. 14: Repeat Measure 13.

Diag. 3

Meas. 15-16: Change back to original positions as in Measures 3 and 4.

Third Figure, Music C

Meas. 17-24: All take ordinary dance position and waltz around the circle, counterclockwise. (See Diagram 4.)

Diag. 4

PEASANT VERSION

Formation: For as many couples as will—in a double circle around the room. Men on the inside of the circle, women on the outside, all facing line of direction (counterclockwise).

Position: Woman is on the man's right. Her left hand rests on man's right shoulder and her right hand is on her right hip. Man's right arm is around his partner's waist; his left hand is on his own left hip.

First Figure, Music A

Meas. 1: Partners take the following three steps (*counts "one—two —three"*). Man begins with the left foot and takes three steps in place (L—R—L). At the same time he swings the woman forward and in front of him, over to his left side, whereupon he places his left arm around her waist. The woman, during this time, takes three steps beginning with the *right* foot (R—L—R), moving forward and in front of man to his left side, turning half left, so that she faces in the same direction as the man. She now places her right hand on his left shoulder.

Meas. 2: Partners place outside heel (man's right, woman's left) to floor and slightly to the side (*count "one"*). Hold (*counts "two— three"*).

Meas. 3: Beginning with the opposite feet (man's right, woman's left) partners change back to original place in the same manner as above. The man swings his partner forward from his left arm to his right arm.

Meas. 4: Place outside heel forward (man's left, woman's right) and to the side, with toes up (*count "one"*). Hold (*counts "two —three"*).

Meas. 5-8: Repeat Measures 1-4.

Second Figure, Music B

Measure 9: Beginning with the outside foot (man's left, woman's right), partners move forward with two walking steps (*counts "one—two"*). Hop on inside foot, raising outside foot (*count "three"*).

Meas. 10: Repeat Measure 9.

Meas. 11-12: Change places as in Measures 1 and 2 of Peasant Version.

Meas. 13-14: Man is now on his partner's right. Repeat Measures 9-10 above, beginning with the outside foot (man's right, woman's left).

Meas. 15-16: Repeat Measures 3-4, changing to original positions.

Third Figure, Music C

Meas. 17-24: Take ordinary dance position and waltz, turning clockwise and moving counterclockwise around the room.

Remember the picture on page 25? Well, here the man leaps in the air in a Polish oberek step to give the illusion that his partner is lifting him!

THE
BAVARIAN LANDLER

EVERYBODY likes to waltz, and the Landler is nothing more than a waltz in figures. The original Bavarian Landler had many complicated figures, usually ending with the traditional *schuplattler*. As time passed by, many of the peasant dances were taken up in modified form by people in towns and cities: this Landler is one of those. The directions give the mechanics of the dance; but like every folk dance, the Landler has a style of its own. To help your group acquire that style, keep the following suggestions in mind.

a) In Figure 1, the joined right hands have a tendency to pull apart as couples turn in place. Try to keep forearms close together from wrist to elbow.

b) In Figure 3, the woman leans back as she turns with partner in place.

c) In Figures 4 and 10, as the woman turns under the man's raised arm, make sure that she dances directly in front of him and not at his side. The couple should progress forward around the circle, the man keeping his partner in front. Instead of the waltz step, the woman may use a pivot step as she turns.

d) In Figures 6 and 8, partners flirt with each other as they kneel or waltz, occasionally exchanging a wink with an adjacent couple.

e) In Figure 9, the window is formed for a purpose: to look at one's partner. This should be done with great flirtation, and perhaps the stealing of a kiss through the opening on the final notes.

f) In Figure 11, the woman looks back over her left and right shoulders as she leads the man on. Sometimes instead of using all eight measures for the waltz forward, she may substitute a four-measure pivot for the last four measures.

g) At the very end of the dance, it is customary for the man to lift his partner high in the air on the last note.

h) Free hands are always kept on the hips. If you ever have an opportunity to witness a real Bavarian demonstration, you will probably observe that the women often keep one hand on the stomach. This gesture is due to the numerous heavy medallions and coins worn on silver chains across their bodices; its purpose is to keep them from bouncing. This is a good point to bring out when teaching the dance. Little gestures like this give each dance its own style and fun.

i) As the music plays, dancers may want to vary the heavy peasant waltz step by keeping time with a series of rhythmic stamps every now and then. That's fine. And there should be lots of loud "yahoos" throughout the dance— the women's high-pitched voices doing most of the yelling.

j) An earthy, peasant style is requisite for the Bavarian Landler.

LÄNDLER

III-IV

V-VI

VII-VIII

IX-X

XI-XII

THE DANCE

Bavarian Couple Dance

Formation: For as many couples as will—around the room.

Music: Play once through as written for the complete dance.

Step: A heavy, peasant waltz step in moderate tempo is used throughout the dance. Accent heavily the first count of each waltz step.

First Figure (Right-hand grasp)

Meas. 1-8: Right hands are clasped at eye level,
with elbows bent at right angle. Free left hands
are kept on the hips. (See Diagram 1.) Couple
waltzes around in place (man begins with the
left foot, woman with the right) swaying slightly from side to side.

Diag. 1

Second Figure (Waltz)

Meas. 1-8 (repeated): Partners take ordinary dance
position and with the same heavy waltz step turn
clockwise and dance counterclockwise around the
room. (See Diagram 2.)

Diag. 2

Third Figure (Cross-hand grasp)

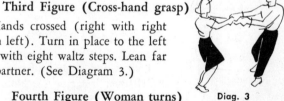

Meas. 9-16: Hands crossed (right with right
and left with left). Turn in place to the left
(clockwise) with eight waltz steps. Lean far
away from partner. (See Diagram 3.)

Fourth Figure (Woman turns)

Diag. 3

Meas. 9-16 (repeated): Man holds right arm high,
as woman grasps one finger of his uplifted hand
with her own right hand. She turns clockwise under the uplifted right hands as the couple dances
counterclockwise around the room. The man follows the woman as she turns, moving forward
and keeping her directly in front of him. Eight
waltz steps in all. (See Diagram 4.)

Diag. 4

Fifth Figure (Back grasp)

Meas. 17-24: Partners hook right elbows, each placing left hand

Diag. 5

behind own back. Woman holds man's left hand with her right and man holds her left with his right. (See Diagram 5.) Make sure elbows are hooked before holding hands. Dance forward in place, turning clockwise with eight waltz steps.

Sixth Figure (Woman kneels)

Meas. 17-24 (repeated): Woman kneels on her right knee, holding man's right hand with her own right hand. Man waltzes clockwise around her with eight waltz steps. (See Diagram 6.)

Diag. 6

Seventh Figure (Neck-waist hold)

Meas. 25-32: Man places both hands on woman's waist, and she clasps both hands on nape of her neck. Couple turns clockwise around the room with eight waltz steps. (See Diagram 7.)

Diag. 7

Eighth Figure (Man kneels)

Meas. 25-32 (repeated): Man kneels on right knee. Partners hold right hands as woman dances clockwise around the man with eight waltz steps. (See Diagram 8.)

Diag. 8

Ninth Figure (Window)

Diag. 9

Meas. 33-40: Partners face each other and join both hands (right with right over left with left; see Diagram 9). Note that with each hand the woman holds the man's middle finger in order to turn easily and to avoid broken wrists. Raise joined hands overhead as in Diagram 9. The woman turns to the right once under the uplifted hands, finishing as in Diagram 10, and then once again (twice in all) finishing as in Diagram 11. Arms will be entangled up above after the second turn. Hang on, and just lower the joined left hands as you bend the right elbows at a right angle. Thus you form a window through which you look at your partner. The man stands still as the woman turns. He does not turn. The foregoing is done in three steps of counts. After the window is formed, continue dancing forward and turning clockwise in place with seven more waltz steps.

Diag. 10	Diag. 11	Diag. 12
(After one turn)	(After two turns)	(Completed window)

Tenth Figure (Unwind and turn)

Meas. 33-40 (*repeated*): Still holding hands, woman turns twice around to the left underneath joined hands (*counts "one—two—three"*). She now reverses her turn, as she releases joined left hands. Couple dances forward, woman turning and man following. Keep free left hands on hips. Seven waltz steps. (See Diagram 4.)

Eleventh Figure (The chase)

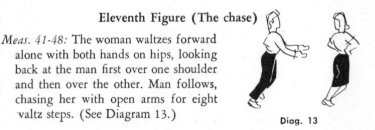

Meas. 41-48: The woman waltzes forward alone with both hands on hips, looking back at the man first over one shoulder and then over the other. Man follows, chasing her with open arms for eight waltz steps. (See Diagram 13.)

Diag. 13

Twelfth Figure (Waltz)

Meas. 41-48 (*repeated*): Partners take ordinary dance positions, and with eight waltz steps turn clockwise and dance counterclockwise around the room. It is customary for the man to lift his partner high in the air on the last note of the music.

THE
SICILIAN TARANTELLA

IT is time for another group dance, one that will restore confidence to those who have had trouble doing the Varsovienne or the Landler. The Sicilian Tarantella is the answer. There are numerous ways of doing the Tarantella, but no other is so simple or so ingratiating as this Sicilian version. Very gay, very flirtatious, lending itself to improvisations, this dance is irresistible—especially when done to the music of native instruments as played on the Victor Sicilianella recording. This record accounts in a good measure for the popularity of the dance; so if you have it, be sure to use it.

Tambourines are optional — the fingers of both hands being snapped instead if they are not used. Some dancers flutter their hands to represent tambourines in Figure 2, but this produces a "hallelujah" effect and makes a burlesque of the dance. Discourage this, in favor of snapping the fingers; discourage also any war-whooping in the dance.

In Figure 1, while the four running steps are made in place, the dancers should avoid swinging their hips too much. Have them snap their fingers or strike their tambourines in front of themselves, not over their heads. In the do-si-do of Figure 4, the dancers should not fold arms across their chests, but should keep snapping fingers as they pass their partners. An extra turn may be added as they return to place. Encourage the dancers to be boldly flirtatious.

The Sicilian Tarantella, high in popularity with folk dancers in every state, can be used successfully with any kind of group.

SICILIAN TARANTELLA

THE DANCE

Italian Group Dance

Formation: For as many as will—in sets of two couples. Partners facing each other. (See Diagram 1.)

Music: Count "one—two" to each measure.

Steps: Hop step, running step, skipping step.

Diag. 1

First Figure

Meas. 1: Step in place with the left foot and clap own hands— women striking their tambourines (*count "one"*). Hop on the left foot, swinging the right across the left (*count "two"*).

Meas. 2: Same as Measure 1, but beginning with the right foot and swinging the left. (See Diagram 1.)

Meas. 3-4: Four running steps in place (L—R—L—R). Men snap their fingers while the women shake their tambourines.

Meas. 5-8: Repeat Measures 1-4.

Meas. 1-8 (repeated): Repeat entire First Figure.

Diag. 2   **Diag. 3**

Second Figure

Meas. 9-10: All take four running steps forward toward partners and bend low (see Diagram 2). Snapping of fingers and shaking of tambourines.

Meas. 11-12: All dance away from partners with four running steps to place, slowly straighten the body, and raise the hands (see Diagram 3). This is accompanied by much snapping of fingers and shaking of tambourines.

Meas. 13-16: Repeat Measures 9-12.

Meas. 9-16 (repeated): Repeat entire Second Figure.

Third Figure

Meas. 17-20: Man of Couple One and woman of Couple Two dance toward each other with a running step and hook right elbows. They turn once around in place clockwise and dance back to their respective positions. (See Diagram 4.)

Diag. 4

Meas. 21-24: Man of Couple Two and woman of Couple One repeat Measures 17-20.

Meas. 17-24 (repeated): Repeat the foregoing, hooking left elbows.

Fourth Figure

Diag. 5

Meas. 1-4: Man of Couple One and woman of Couple Two dance around each other passing right shoulders, and returning backward to place passing left shoulders (do-si-do). (See Diagram 5.)

Meas. 5-8: Man of Couple Two and woman of Couple One do the same.

Meas. 1-8 (repeated): Same as the foregoing; this time pass by the left shoulder going forward and by the right shoulder returning.

Fifth Figure

Meas. 9-12: All place hands on their own hips and face the right, with left shoulders in the center of the set. (See Diagram 6.) All take eight skipping steps counterclockwise.

Meas. 13-16: All turn halfway to the left. Now with right shoulder to the center they take eight skipping steps clockwise back to original place.

Sixth Figure

Meas. 9-12 (repeated): All place left hands in the center of the set, forming a left-hand star (see Diagram 7), and take eight skipping steps counterclockwise. The women shake their tambourines.

Diag. 6   **Diag. 7**

Meas. 13-16 (repeated): All drop joined hands and turn halfway to the left, placing right hands in the center of the set (right-hand star). All dance with eight skipping steps clockwise to place.

Repeat as many times as desired.

just plain folks of all nationalities doing a Jugoslav "Kolo"—a circle dance requiring no partners. You merely improvise on a basic step throughout the dance. This is one dance we recommend learning through actual experience rather than through a book because it is full of elusive syncopated bounces and rhythms. The plaid-shirted figure in the center is Gjon Mili, photographer for this book and an expert Kolo dancer.

This position from the Swedish "Varsovienne" is found in many other folk dances. The costumes shown here have bright red as the predominating color.

NOTE

BY this time your group has done nine dances,
which is the maximum number that can be
absorbed well by any group in one session. It is a good idea to in-
sert plain waltzes, polkas, or schottisches as "rest-period" dances
in between the teaching. When going on to a second session on
another day, repeat some of the dances done at the previous session, especially those that took a little more time to learn. And
add a few new ones, such as those found in the next section of
this book. A good setup is to devote two-thirds of an evening to
teaching new dances and to devote the last third to a review of
the dances taught in the previous session—with no, or a mini-
mum amount of, leading.

THE
DANISH TO TING

INCORPORATING a waltz step and a walking
step, this simple Danish dance is aptly suited as
one of those folk dances that find their way onto the ballroom
floor during social evenings. Often you will find the To Ting
("Two Things") done at Scandinavian restaurants as casually as
the fox trot.

Participants should keep free hands on hips, as in other Danish
dances, and should move forward in the open waltz position.

TO TING

THE DANCE

Danish Couple Dance

Formation: A couple dance for as many as will. Partners stand side by side—the man on the left of the woman, holding her left hand in his right. The outside hands are placed on the hips. (See Diagram 1.)

Diag. 1

First Figure

Meas. 1-4: Open waltz, beginning with the outside foot (man's left, woman's right). Waltz forward, balancing slightly away from partner on the first step and in on the second step, etc. (See Diagram 1.)

Meas. 5-8: Take ordinary dance position, and with four waltz steps turn clockwise and dance counter-clockwise around the room. (See Diagram 2.)

Meas. 1-8 (repeated): Repeat the above.

Diag. 2

Second Figure

Meas. 9-12: Partners place outside hands on hips (man's left, woman's right; see Diagram 3). All take four walking steps in line of direction (counterclockwise) beginning with the outside foot (man's left, woman's right).

Diag. 3

Meas. 13-16: Man grasps partner's waist with both hands; she places both hands upon his shoulders. Partners turn clockwise with four walking steps or pivot. (See Diagram 4.)

Meas. 9-16 (repeated): Repeat Second Figure.

Diag. 4

THE
SWISS WEGGIS

THE schottische step is found in a great many folk dances. In place of teaching the step alone, however, it is better to teach it as a part of a dance. The Swiss Weggis is a good one to use for this purpose, since the schottische step is repeated five times as a part of its chorus.

The Weggis, also known under the names of "Auf der Landstrasse," "Swiss Walking Song," "Holdiridia," etc., might almost be called an American dance, for it was created in New York by the Swiss group in preparation for a folk dance presentation at the New School for Social Research. Authentic figures from different cantons were put together to make up the Weggis, which now outranks in popularity dances that really originated in Switzerland.

The version here given is the dance as done by the Swiss Folk Dancers of New York, Robin Witschi leader.

Swiss dances are usually done at a moderate tempo, with only occasional fast movements. Although they are precise, in the manner of Scandinavian dances, they have more freedom in pattern. Their flirtatious quality is not too obvious; nothing wild or fierce marks Swiss dances; they are rather a combination of dignity and sly fun.

Yodeling should be encouraged during the chorus. (There are available many good Swiss yodeling records which can be used to study the different types of yodels.) The music itself is an old folk song which has many available English translations. For those who would like to sing as they dance, here is one version:

From Lucerne to Weggis oh,
Hol-di-ri-di-a, hol-di-ri-a,
Shoes nor stockings need we own,
Hol-di-ri-di-a, hol-di-a.

Chorus:
Hol-di-ri-di-a
Hol-di-ri-di-a, hol-di-ri-a
Hol-di-ri-di-a
Hol-di-ri-di-a, hol-di-a.

On the lake we all shall go,
Hol-di-ri-di-a, hol-di-ri-a,
See the pretty fish below,
Hol-di-ri-di-a, hol-di-a.
Chorus.

Weggis starts the highest hill,
Hol-di-ri-di-a, hol-di-ri-a,
Boys and girls, shout "hop-sa-saa,"
Hol-di-ri-di-a, hol-di-a.
Chorus.

Many folk dances provide two women for one man, a situation the men enjoy, to be sure! In this Finnish dance, however, the odd man seeks to lure one of the women off by executing some special steps in front of them.

WEGGIS

INTRO. and INTERLUDE

FIGURE

CHORUS

THE DANCE

Swiss Couple Dance

Formation: For any number of couples—facing counterclockwise in a double circle around the room. Man has partner on his right.

Music: Play introduction before each figure; this acts as an interlude during which partners assume new positions for the next figure. Count "one—and—two—and" to each measure.

Steps: Walking step, hop step, schottische step, and polka step.

First Figure

Meas. 1: All place left heels to floor diagonally forward left (*count "one"*; see Diagram 1.) Touch left toe to floor a little in front of right toe (*count "two"*). (See Diagram 2.)

Diag. 1   Diag. 2

Meas. 2: One polka step diagonally forward left; hop on the right foot (*count "and"* of Measure 1); step forward on the left foot (*count "one"*); bring right foot to left (*count "and"*). Step forward on left foot (*count "two"*). Pause (*count "and"*). Whenever "polka step" is mentioned, do the step in the same manner.

Meas. 3-4: Repeat Measures 1-2, beginning with the right foot and moving diagonally forward right.

Meas. 1-4 (repeated): Repeat Measures 1-4.

Chorus

Diag. 3

Meas. 5: All place both hands on own hips. Partners take one schottische step sidewards away from each other—the man to his left, toward the center of the set (L—R—L—hop); the woman to her right away from the center (R—L—R—hop). (See Diagram 3.) Do not swing leg, but keep free foot under body when doing the hop.

Diag. 4

Meas. 6: All take one sideward schottische step back to partners (man R—L—R—hop; woman L—R—L—hop). Partners face each other and take shoulder-waist position. (See Diagram 4.)

Meas. 7-8: Couples turn clockwise with four hop steps (man begins with the left foot, woman with the right foot).

Meas. 5-8 (repeated): Repeat Chorus.

Second Figure

Formation: Partners join hands and assume position in which the man's left shoulder and the woman's right are toward the center of the room or circle. Inside hands point downward; outside hands are up, with arms of partners held close together at shoulder level and bent at the elbow. (See Diagram 5.)

Diag. 5

Meas. 1-2: Touch heel and toe as in First Figure; this time the man begins with the left foot and the woman with the right. Take one polka step forward toward the center of the circle.

Meas. 3-4: Partners turn in place slightly, to face away from the center. Do not release hands! Change position of the hands, always lowering them in the direction of the movement. Do heel and toe and polka step, as in Measures 1-2, back to original places.

Meas. 1-4 (repeated): Repeat the foregoing.

Meas. 5-8 (repeated twice): Repeat Chorus.

Third Figure

Diag. 6

Meas. 1: Facing counterclockwise, all take crossed-hands position. (See Diagram 6.) Both man and partner step to the side, swinging the left foot to the left in a half arc (*count "one"*). Swing the right foot across and in front of the left; touch right toe to floor close to left toe (*count "two"*). (See Diagram 6.)

Meas. 2: Step to the right in the same manner, starting with the right foot.

Meas. 3-4: All take two polka steps forward in line of direction (counterclockwise).

Meas. 1-4 (*repeated*): Repeat the foregoing.

Meas. 5-8 (*repeated twice*): Repeat Chorus.

Fourth Figure

Formation: Partners face each other, with joined right hands held high in arch. Man's back to the center of the circle. (See Diagram 7.)

Meas. 1-2: Same step as in Measures 1-2 of Third Figure.

Meas. 3-4: Partners take two polka steps forward, moving clockwise into partner's position.

Meas. 1-4: (*repeated*): Repeat the foregoing returning to original places.

Meas. 5-8 (*repeated twice*): Repeat Chorus.

Diag. 7   Diag. 8   Diag. 9

Fifth Figure

Formation: Partners join inside hands (man's right, woman's left), holding them well back at shoulder level and facing each other. (See Diagram 8.)

Meas. 1-2: Man begins with left foot, woman with right. Partners take three walking steps forward in circle (counterclockwise), turning once around away from each other (man to the left; woman to the right). (See Diagram 9.) Swing the hands downward and forward at beginning of the turn and release for the turn (*counts "one—two—one"*). Join other hands, face partner, and bow and curtsy (*count "two"*).

 Meas. 3-4: Man begins with right foot, woman with left. All take three steps back to place (clockwise). Turn away from partner (man to right, woman to left) and release hands. Join other hands. Bow and curtsy. (See Diagram 10.)

Diag. 10   *Meas. 1-4:* (*repeated*): As above.

Meas. 5-8 (repeated twice): Repeat Chorus.

* * *

The dance should be progressive. The change is made during the second half of the Chorus. When Measures 5-8 are repeated for the second time, partners dance away from each other with one sideward schottische step. In Measures 7-8 the man takes one schottische step to the right and forward, taking for his new partner the woman ahead; the woman takes one schottische step to the left and assumes shoulder-waist position with man of the couple behind her. New partners should be had for each figure.

The Polish dance demonstrated here by Bronislaw Matuz, leader of the Polish Folk Dance Circle, and his partner is on the vigorous and difficult side. It's nice to watch, but we don't recommend it for general folk dance purposes.

THE
RUSSIAN KOHANOCHKA

THERE is a big difference (even in costume) between Russian peasant dances and Russian ballroom dances; and when teaching or doing Russian dances, one must keep this difference in mind.

The peasant dances are marked by complicated figures, vigorous movements, and heavy steps—including notably the *prysiadka* (squat step). This latter step is not found in any of the dances in the present book; but remarks about it are pertinent, in order that it will not by any chance find its way into the Russian ballroom dance. In Russia the *prysiadka* is used to give the man a chance to demonstrate his physical prowess; it is never done by a woman (if she dared to do it, she would undoubtedly lose all respect in her community). In this country members of the fair sex should be cautioned not only that it is an ungainly step, but that it deflates the men's egos.

Unlike the peasant dances, Russian ballroom dances are smooth, graceful, and comparatively simple. There are many of them, such as the Karapiet (Two-step), Koroboushka, Espan, Pas-d' Espan, Hiavata, and the Kohanochka here given. Because there is a certain amount of similarity between all of them, it is important to retain the original authentic form of each. The addition of extra turns, claps, or stamps erases the individuality and makes them all feel and look alike.

The Kohanochka ("Beloved") is a good, representative dance of the type. The whole spirit of the Kohanochka should be one of constant flowing movement forward. (Sometimes dancers want to do a *pas de bas* in place, instead of moving forward; but the *pas de bas* destroys the style of this dance.) In the third figure, note that partners do not pass as in the American do-si-do—but pass each time by the left shoulder, keeping the woman first in respect to the line of direction. Pay special attention to the use of the free hands as described in the directions.

KOHANOCHKA

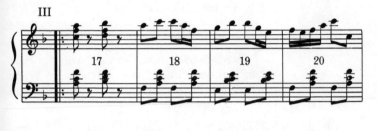

THE DANCE

Russian Couple Dance

Formation: A double circle around the room—men on the inside, women on the outside. Partners have inside hands joined and outside hands swinging freely at the side.

First Figure

Meas. 1: Couples dance forward with one balance polka step (known also as the Russian polka), beginning with the outside foot (man's left, woman's right). They move forward smoothly, without hopping. All swing joined, inside hands forward at shoulder level and swing free, outside hands back gracefully at the same time. (See Diagram 1.)

Diag. 1

MAN'S STEP: Step forward with the left foot (*count "one"*), close right foot up to the left foot (*count "and"*), step forward with the left foot (*count "two"*), and pause (*count "and"*).

WOMAN'S STEP: Same as the man's, but with opposite feet.

Meas. 2: All dance one polka step forward beginning with the inside foot (man's right and woman's left). All swing joined inside hands back (keep hands at shoulder level) and outside hands gracefully across the chest at the same time. (See Diagram 2.)

MAN'S STEP: Step forward with the right foot (*count "one"*), close left foot up to the right (*count "and"*), step forward with the right foot (*count "two"*), and pause (*count "and"*).

Diag. 2

WOMAN'S STEP: Same as the man's, but with opposite feet.

Meas. 3-4: All swing joined inside hands forward. Release hands and beginning with the outside foot, take two polka steps forward for one complete turn away from partner. (See Diagram 3.)

MAN'S STEP: Man turns to the left away from partner, making one complete turn with two balance polka steps, beginning with the left foot and progressing forward in the line of direction (counter-clockwise).

Diag. 3

WOMAN'S STEP: Woman turns to the right, away from partner, to do the same beginning with the right foot.

Meas. 5-8: Repeat Measures 1-4.

Second Figure

Meas. 9: Partners take the following position: Woman is on the man's right. The man's right arm is extended behind (across) his partner's shoulders so that his right hand holds her raised right hand. Her left arm is stretched out in front of the man's chest, and her left hand rests in his left hand. (See Diagram 4.) Couples balance by stepping forward

Diag. 4

onto the left foot and lifting the right foot (at the same time), keeping it well under the body.

Meas. 10: Couples balance by stepping back onto the right foot and lifting the left foot at the same time.

Meas. 11-12: Couples take two balance polka steps forward (counterclockwise), beginning with the left foot.

Meas. 13-16: Repeat Measures 9-12

Third Figure

Meas. 17: Partners face each other (man's back to the center of the circle), and all clap own hands twice.

Meas. 18-20: All dance backwards away from partner with three balance polka steps (man to the center of the circle, woman away from the center). Man's arms are crossed on his chest, woman's hands are on her hips.

Meas. 21: All clap own own hands twice more.

Meas. 22-24: All dance forward (toward partner) with three polka steps, passing each other by the left shoulder.

Meas. 17-24 (repeated):

Meas. 17: All clap own hands twice while standing in place.

Meas. 18-20: All dance backwards to original positions with three balance polka steps, passing partners by the left shoulder.

Meas. 21: All clap own hands twice more.

Meas. 22: Pause, all standing motionless in place.

Meas. 23-24: All take two polka steps forward in line of direction (counter-clockwise), making one complete turn away from partner. (See Diagram 3.)

Repeat the dance from the beginning as many times as desired.

THE AMERICAN
RED RIVER VALLEY

RED RIVER VALLEY is usually a square dance; but in West Virginia it is done as a play-party game, with the different and interesting form given here. This version comes from Jane Farwell, who headed the Folk Dance Camps held at Oglebay Park in Wheeling.

You don't even need music to do this dance, since everyone can sing the words which tell what to do. Although traditionally performed with one man and two women in each set of three, the dance can also be performed with one woman and two men. (The sets must be consistent, however, to avoid confusion.) If two men are used, the words should be adapted to fit the situation, "Red River Gal" becoming "Red River Man," etc.

In teaching the dance, make sure that everyone thoroughly understands the first figure; have all sets do it several times before leading to the next figure.

In doing line two of each verse, "circle to the left and to the right," tell the group not to be too slow about veering to the right, or else they will change direction too late to return to place for the action of the figure. In the second verse, the ladies must step lively in the "wheel" in order to get back in time to give the men space for the do-si-do.

It is not compulsory to use all three figures of the dance. Sometimes when the group is slow at catching on, the first figure may be repeated over and over again. Or just the first and second or first and third figures may be combined. The important thing is to have the dancers sing "good and loud."

RED RIVER VALLEY

THE DANCE

American Progressive Play Party

Song

Verse 1: Now you lead right down to the valley,
And you circle to the left and to the right.
Now you swing with the girl in the valley,
And you swing with your Red River Girl.

Verse 2: Now you lead right down to the valley,
And you circle to the left and to the right.
Now the girls make a wheel in the valley,
And the boys do-si-do so polite.

Verse 3: Now you lead right down to the valley,
And you circle to the left and to the right.
Now you lose your girl in the valley,
And you lose your Red River Girl.

Diag. 1

Formation: Each man has a woman on either side for his partners. Each set of three faces another set of three. (See Diagram 1.)

Verse 1: With hands joined, players walk diagonally forward to the right, passing the opposite set and facing a new set. (See Diagram 2.)

Diag. 2

On reaching the new set, all six join hands in a single circle and walk four steps to the left and four steps to the right.

Each man swings his right hand partner while the left one stands still. (See Diagram 3.)

Each man swings his left hand partner while the right one stands still.

Diag. 3

Diag. 4

Verse 2: Each set passes the opposite and faces another set.

On reaching the new set, all six join hands and walk, as above, to the left and to the right.

The four women form a right hand star and walk eight steps clockwise; then back to place. (See Diagram 4.)

The two men dance around each other, passing right shoulders, and returning backward to place passing left shoulders. (Do-si-do; see Diagram 5.)

Verse 3: All sets of three walk to the right, passing the opposite set and joining a new one.

Diag. 5

The six join hands to form a circle which walks first to the left and then to the right.

The right-hand women change places.

The left-hand women change places. Thus each man has two new partners with whom to proceed as the dance is done over again.

THE
UKRAINIAN OHORODNIK

AT the end of Red River Valley, the dancers are grouped in sets of three, and it is easy to lead them into the Ukrainian Ohorodnik — which can utilize the same sets, but in a square formation.

Because the more intricate and strenuous dances of the Ukraine are the ones usually chosen for demonstration, few people know that there are also Ukrainian dances which are simple. Actually, however, the Ohorodnik ("Gardener") is more typical of a community gathering in the Ukraine than are some of the difficult dances such as the Hopak and the Kolomeyka.

Although the first part of the dance is done to a moderate tempo, the second part is extremely fast and here the Ukrainian flavor is retained by having the women do the "work." The man does not turn his women partners (as is customary in the dances of most countries), but rather they turn him. The first woman runs forward towards the man, hooks elbows with him, and turns him around in his place; before he can recover, the second woman hooks his other elbow and spins him around. The idea is to keep the center person revolving in one spot.

As in other dances using a "threes" formation, adjustment can be made to fit the occasion by grouping one woman with two men.

The Ohorodnik is especially popular with Ukrainians in the Woonsocket, R. I., area where it is often danced at weddings.

OHORODNIK

THE DANCE
Ukrainian Group Dance

Formation: A dance for twelve people in square formation. Sets of three (one man and two women) on each side of a square.

First Figure

Meas. 1-2: Sets One and Three dance forward toward each other with six running steps. (See Diagram 1.)

Diag. 1

Meas. 3-4: Sets One and Three dance backwards to place with six running steps. At the same time Sets Two and Four dance forward toward each other with six running steps.

Meas. 5-6: Sets Two and Four dance backwards to place while Sets One and Three dance forward toward the center. Six running steps for each set.

Meas. 7-8: Sets One and Three dance backwards to place while Sets Two and Four dance forward.

Meas. 1-8 (repeated): As in the above eight measures.

Second Figure

Diag. 2

Meas. 9-10: The right-hand woman hooks right elbows with the man in her set and turns him once around with four fast running steps. (See Diagram 2.)

Meas. 11-12: The woman on the man's left hooks left elbows with him and turns him once around with four more running steps.

Meas. 13-16: As in Meas. 9-12.

Meas. 9-16 (repeated): As above.

The "Grand Right and Left" is another common figure found in folk dances of many lands, but especially in the American square. Here a Norwegian group shows how they put their own individual stamp on this figure by holding their hands high in the air as they pass each other around the set.

Here's the American "swing your partner" figure which is so similar to the Finnish one found on page 11. Many of the European folk dances bear such a striking resemblance to American squares that were it not for the costumes and the titles, one could easily be passed off for the other.

THE
ITALIAN DANZA

THE Danza is a slow, dignified dance full of grace and charm. Originally it was a court dance done by the nobility in northern Italy. Peasants, watching the nobles through the castle gates, began imitating them and thus creating their own version. The courtly poses are evident throughout the dance—with stately attitudes and polite bows all slightly exaggerated, as if making fun of the nobility. The exuberance of the peasant cannot be restrained for long, however, and the dancers break into a lively hop step in the last figure.

This background picture should be imparted to your group, so that they can fully enjoy the dance and give it its proper character. Ask the women to curtsy deeply, and the men to bow low with sweeping motions of the arms. The more pomp and ceremony during the bows, the better.

The Tarantella is, of course, the dance most often identified with the Italians. One of its many versions is given elsewhere in this book. But just as spaghetti is not the only food Italians eat, neither is the Tarantella the only dance they know. Utilizing the Danza in your folk dance program will give your group another aspect of Italian character—their love of mimicry.

The music for the dance is quite tuneful, often invoking the men to whistle as they dance.

The Danza was first introduced by the Coro D'Italia of New York.

DANZA

♩ = 66

INTRO.

Fig. 1

Fig. 2

♩ = 72

THE DANCE

Italian

Formation: Couples in a circle all facing counter-clockwise—men on the inside, women on the outside.

Position: Side-cross-grasp: standing side by side, partners join both hands, right with right and left with left. It is important to keep joined right hands underneath joined left hands. (See Diagram 1.) In "front cross-grasp" partners face each other.

Diag. 1

First Figure

Meas. 1: Couples step forward with the right foot (*count "one"*). Bring left foot up to the right (*count "and"*). Step forward again onto the right foot (*count "two"*), bringing left foot up to the right (*count "and"*).

Meas. 2: Step forward once more with the right foot (*count "one"*). All pause (*count "and"*). Point left toe forward in front of the right (*count "two"*) and hold (*count "and"*). (See Diagram 2.)

Meas. 3-4: Repeat Measures 1-2 beginning with the left foot. Finish with the right foot forward in the point as in Diagram 1.

Diag. 2

Meas. 5: All step back on the right foot (*count "one"*). Pause (*count "and"*). Point with the left toe diagonally forward (*count "two"*). Pause (*count "and"*).

Meas. 6: All step back on the left foot (*count "one"*). Pause (*count "and"*). Point right toe forward (*count "two"*). Pause (*count "and"*).

Meas. 7-8: Continue as in Measures 5 and 6.

Meas. 1-8 (repeated): As above.

Second Figure

Diag. 3

Meas. 9-10: Partners face each other and raise joined hands to form an arch. The man does not turn, but the woman turns completely around to her left (see Diagram 3) under crossed uplifted arms, in place. To do this she takes three slow walking steps on *counts "one—two"* of Measure 9 and *count "one"* of Measure 10.

Partners drop joined hands. The man bows while the woman curtsies (*counts "two—and"* of Measure 10; see Diagram 4).

Diag. 4

Meas. 11-12: Join hands again in a "front cross-grasp," bearing in mind that right hands are underneath the left. Partners change places with three walking steps. The woman turns once around to the left (as in the preceding measure) in the change, and walks to man's position. The man does not turn but walks forward (to woman's position) to his right as they change. It is to be noted that the woman is first in respect to the line of direction. All drop joined hands and bow as before.

Diag. 5

Meas. 13-14: Partners give right hand to each other with free hand on hip or holding skirt. Partners change places with three slow walking steps, the woman turning to the left under joined right hands during the change. (See Diagram 5.) The man walks to his left back to his original position (*counts "one—and—two—and"* of Measure 13 and *counts "one—and"* of Measure 14). All drop hands, bow and curtsy on *counts "two—and"* of Measure 14.

Meas. 15-16: Joining left hands, partners change places again with three slow walking steps, the woman turning once around to her right under joined left hands in the change. The man walks forward to his right to the woman's position. (See Diagram 6.)

Diag. 6

Third Figure

Meas. 9-10 (repeated): Partners hook right elbows and change places with three walking steps. Bow, curtsy as before. (See Diagram 7.)

Meas. 11-12: Hooking left elbows, partners change places once more with three slow walking steps. Bow as before.

Diag. 7   Diag. 8

Meas. 13-16: Couples take ordinary dance position and turn clockwise (see Diagram 8), taking eight hop steps. Move counterclockwise around the circle while turning. Man begins by stepping on his left foot, woman on her right foot. Finish by taking original crossed-hands position, ready for the repetition of the dance.

Repeat as many times as desired.

THE
POLISH KUJAWIAK

THE dances from here on are more advanced. They are not at all in the category of difficult dances, but they are less quickly learned than those on the preceding pages. They are suitable for you to use as "feature" dances at your sessions, spending more time on them than you would on the others; or else you can devote several sessions to teaching them.

The Polish people have a great variety of dances, ranging in mood from the very slow and dreamy to the sprightly, nimble Krakowiak and Mazur and the stately Polonaise. The Kujawiak is done in various ways in different parts of Poland. The version given here is one of the simpler ones. It was introduced by the Polish Folk Arts and Dance Group of New York, John Galinski leader.

More than any other, this dance requires good style; otherwise it doesn't give the dancers any pleasure. The style is quite different from that of other folk dances. The hands should sweep slowly, the body bend gracefully, the whole bearing be one of elegance. The music is played in very slow tempo for the first part, with only a slight acceleration and a slight increased accent in the second part.

The first figure, which is just a walking step forward, should be described as a stroll with couples imagining themselves in a shady lane and the full moon overhead. They whisper to each other, pointing out passing scenes with their free hands as they stroll.

The figures of the Kujawiak are simple. It is the chorus that will require concentration. Make sure that everyone starts the chorus with the inside foot on count "one" and leaps on count "two." The rest will come easily.

KUJAWIAK

THE DANCE

Polish

Formation: A couple dance for as many as will in a double circle around the room. Men on the inside, women on the outside. Man's right arm around his partner's waist, her left hand on man's right shoulder. Outside hands swing freely. (See Diagram 1.)

First Figure

Diag. 1

Meas. 1-4: Couples walk forward in the line of direction (counter-clockwise) with slow walking steps, one step for each count.

Meas. 1-4 (repeated): As above.

Chorus

Diag. 2

Meas. 5: Partners join inside hands and hold out-side hands gracefully to the side and backward. All take one step forward on the inside foot (man's right, woman's left) in line of direc-tion (counterclockwise; *count "one"*). (See Diagram 2.) On *count "two,"* partners step on the outside foot (man's left, woman's right) turning towards each other at the same time so that his foot is in the same place that the other foot (inside) was on *count "one,"* but pointing in the opposite direction (clock-wise; see Diagram 3). Bodies are bent at the waist, knees are bent, and dancers are facing clockwise. In mov-

Diag. 3

ing from *count "one"* to *count "two,"* bring the outside hands in a graceful, sweeping motion across the chest. (See Diagram 3.) On *count "three"* all step in place with the free foot (man's right, woman's left) slowly straighten-ing up and turning to face the original direction (counterclockwise).

Diag. 4

Meas. 6: All take three walking steps forward in line of direction (counterclockwise) beginning with the man's left, woman's right. Gradually bring joined inside hands up to shoulder level, as outside hands slowly swing backward and upward ending in a back to back position. (See Diagram 4.) There should be a graceful curve from the top of the outside hands to the joined inside hands.

Meas. 7-8: As in Measures 5 and 6 except that on the last count the pose is held in a retard with the weight on the outside foot (which should be placed slightly in front of the inside foot). (See Dia-gram 4.)

Meas. 5-8 (repeated): As above.

Second Figure

Meas. 1: Partners join both hands, man's right with woman's left and his left with her right.

Diag. 5

A very slow balance waltz step to the man's left. (See Diagram 5.)

Meas. 2: Balance waltz step to the man's right.

Meas. 3-4: Two slow waltz steps turning toward the man's left, underneath joined hands, and once around. (This is sometimes known as the "wring the dishrag" figure; see Diagram 6.)

Meas. 1-4 (repeated): As above.

Meas. 5-8 (repeated twice): Chorus.

Diag. 6

Third Figure

Meas. 1-2: In ordinary dance position, partners take two slow waltz steps turning clockwise (once around) and moving counterclockwise around the room.

Meas. 3: Man takes his right arm away from his partner's waist as she turns clockwise (to her right) once around and forward in a circle under her raised right arm. (See Diagram 7.)

Diag. 7

Meas. 4: Man turns to the left (counterclockwise) once around under his uplifted left arm and forward in line of direction following his partner.

Meas. 1-4 (repeated): As above.

Meas. 5-8 (repeated twice): Chorus.

THE
ESTONIAN EIDE RATAS

ESTONIA — tiny country that she is — has produced a good many popular folk dances: the Jamaja Labajalg, the Viru Waltz, the Vandra Polka, the Tuljak, the Tilut-Tilut, etc. The Eide Ratas ("Spinning Wheel") has a haunting melody which no doubt contributes a great deal to its popularity.

It is important that the first step (the leap and bend of Measures 1 and 2) be thoroughly mastered, for it is a distinguishing characteristic of this Estonian dance. Be sure to keep the outside hand on the hip during the spinning figure in the second part. Putting it in the air would give the dance a non-Estonian flavor. If you like to sing as you dance, here are the words:

Come and dance, dance to
  vo-ki-ra-tas,

Ketra, ketra, ketra ei-de-ra-tas

Singing as we trip along,

Come and join our spinning
  song.

Chorus:

Sing lerie, lerie, lee-oh

Sing lerie, lerie, lay-oh,

Turn, turn my spinning wheel,

Lerie, lee-rie, lay-oh.

(Words by permission of Andrew Scarlett.)

The dance was first introduced by the Estonian Educational Society of New York, directed by Mrs. Alice Zimmerman.

EIDE RATAS

THE DANCE

Estonian Couple Dance

Formation: For as many couples as will in ordinary dance position facing counterclockwise.

First Figure

Diag. 1

Meas. 1: Beginning with the outside foot (man's left, woman's right), partners take two walking steps forward (*counts "one—two"*). Hop on the inside foot (*count "three"*).

N.B. After mastering this basic step, proceed to do the step thereafter in the following way, which is the correct one to use. Leap onto the outside foot (*count "one"*) bending the body forward at the same time. (See Diagram 1.) Step on the inside foot (*count "two"*), hop on the inside foot (*count "three"*) straightening the body at the same time.

Meas. 2: Repeat Measure 1.

Meas. 3-4: Couples turn clockwise once around with six running steps.

Meas. 5-8: Repeat Measures 1-4.

Meas. 1-8 (*repeated*): Repeat as above.

Second Figure

Partners face each other with hands on own hips. Men on the inside facing outward, women on the outside facing the center.

Diag. 2

Meas. 9: Beginning with the left foot, partners make a half left turn with three steps. (See Diagram 2.) They move away from each other going backwards.

Meas. 10: Beginning with the right foot, partners make a half right turn for three more steps, still moving away from each other.

Meas. 11-12: Repeat Measures 9-10.

Diag. 3   Diag. 4

Meas. 13-16: Partners run forward toward each other. (See Diagram 3.) On meeting they hook right elbows and turn in place, spinning clockwise with twelve running steps in all. (See Diagram 4.) They finish in each other's places. Now the man is on the outside of the circle facing in.

Meas. 9-16 (*repeated*): Repeat the above. In Measures 13-16 the partners hook left elbows and finish in their original positions, ready to repeat the dance from the beginning.

Repeat Figures 1 and 2 for Measures 17-32.

THE
GERMAN KREUZ KOENIG

AFTER your group of folk dancers are going full swing and have mastered well the preceding dances, you can reward them by teaching the Kreuz Koenig. It is the dance that everyone from coast to coast wants to learn at the start. It isn't too difficult, but at the same time it isn't easy; and it does require a little more work and concentration than any of the preceding dances. Most leaders would hesitate to teach it to a group that had never folk danced before.

Although the following directions give all the necessary details, attention should be called to the Fifth Figure. In order to preserve the pattern of this figure, the center dancers, women or men, must be careful to remain back to back and the outside dancers to keep their arms stretched out straight. This figure can be quite confusing. The secret to emphasize is this: *Never let go your partner's right hand* throughout the figure.

In their enthusiasm for this dance, some groups use a fast running step in the Second Figure which tends to sweep the end girls off their feet. Dancers should be cautioned against this and told to use a leisurely running step instead.

In playing the music watch the change of tempos for each figure as marked by the metronome readings.

Kreuz Koenig is of German origin and the name means "King of Clubs." The dance is here taught as done by Ann German of New Jersey.

KREUZ KOENIG

THE DANCE

German Group Dance

Diag. 1

Formation: Sets of two couples. Hands joined in a circle with the woman on the man's right, and all facing the center of the set. (See Diagram 1.)

First Figure

Meas. 1-2: All leap on left foot to the side (*count "one"*), place right foot back of left (*count "two"; see Diagram 1*), turn half left, and take four running steps forward (clockwise; *counts "three—one—two—three"*).

Meas. 3-8: Continue as in Measures 1-2, three more times.

Second Figure

Meas. 1-8 (repeated): The two men hook left elbows with right arms around partner's waist. Each holds left hand of opposite woman (with own left hand) behind other man's back. (See Diagram 2.) All run forward (counterclockwise) with 24 running steps.

Diag. 2

Third Figure

Meas. 9-12: All release hands and the two couples face each other. Men join left hands (see Diagram 3) and with a hop step (one to each measure) pass each other. Then they give their right hands to the opposite woman, turning once around with her. Four hop steps in all.

Diag. 3

Meas. 13-14: Men join left hands once more and pass each other by the left shoulder with two hop steps.

Meas. 15: Partners join right hands—woman turns clockwise under uplifted right hands while the man stands motionless.

Meas. 16: Partners bow and curtsy.

Meas. 9-16 (repeated): As above.

Fourth Figure

Meas. 17: The two couples join hands in circle formation and dance forward in line of direction (clockwise) with the following step: Step forward on the left foot (*count "one"*), step forward on the right foot (*count "two"*), hop on the right foot while raising left foot (*count "three"*). This is called the L—R hop. (See Diagram 4.)

Diag. 4

Meas. 18-20: Repeat measure 17 three more times.

Meas. 21-22: Release hands in the circle formation. Partners join both hands and turn clockwise in place with the same step, done twice. (L—R hop and L—R hop; see Diagram 5.)

Meas. 23-24: Partners finish the figure with six running steps, turning in place clockwise.

Meas. 17-24 (repeated): Repeat as above.

Diag. 5

Fifth Figure

Meas. 25-28: Men hold right hands of partners and swing partners to the center of the set. The women in the center are back to back. All give left hands to the opposites. THROUGHOUT THIS FIGURE, NEVER LET GO RIGHT HANDS. Men run to the left with twelve steps. Women run in place, kicking feet slightly forward. (See Diagram 6.)

Diag. 6

Meas. 29: Men release the hand of the opposite woman, keeping right hands joined with partner. Men swing women to the outside as they move into the center of the set (see Diagram 7), finishing in back to back position. Men join left hands with the opposite and finish as in Diagram 8. Three running steps are used in making this change.

Diag. 7

Meas. 30-32: With the men on the inside and women on the outside, men run in place while the women run to the left (clockwise). (See Diagram 8.)

Meas. 25-32 (repeated): As above.

The dance is repeated with a different partner in this manner. At the conclusion of the Fifth Figure with men in the center back to back, all release

Diag. 8

joined hands. The men turn in place to face the center of the set. All join hands in a circle. The men will find their old partner on the left and a new partner on the right. Do the dance over again with the new partner.

Sweden, too, likes square dances. What makes them fun to do are the occasional odd gestures and positions like those demonstrated here by the Swedish Folk Dance Society of New York.

Most Ukrainian dances are too difficult for general recreation purposes. Ukrainian costumes, however, are quite colorful. These are good examples of the mountaineer's costume except for the satin trousers which really should be made of red wool. Though satin looks better than wool under stage lights, the change to it should be avoided if one wishes to be authentic. The footwear is not meant to be ballet slippers. They are the type of moccasin worn by Ukrainian mountaineers.

THE FINNISH
TRIP TO HELSINKI

G OOD for finishing up a session is the longways
dance from Finland, A Trip to Helsinki. Here
again is a dance that can be used at any time with any kind of
group, and one that is guaranteed to provide fun for the participants.

The dance depicts a trip to the nation's capitol. The last figure
demonstrates the hills and vales one has to go through to reach
Helsinki. Here are the words to sing with the music.

Come go with me to Helsinki,

Hei la la la la, Hei la la la la.

Happy the trip will surely be,

Hei la la la la, Hei la la la la.

Now then if you'll bow,
  then I will curtsy,

Now let's turn to go, let's turn
  together.

Now to Helsinki we will go,

Hei la la la la, Hei la la la la,

Happy the trip will be I know,

Hei la la la la, Hei la la la la.

Since the chorus is repeated after each figure, it is better to teach
it first and then to show each figure separately. As the dancers
take the last trip to Helsinki, after everyone has had a chance
to lead, the line trips right off the floor, with everyone following
the leaders as they wind their way in whatever direction they
choose to go.

In America the dance was first taught by William Hynynen to
the Finnish Folk Dance Group of Imatra, directed by Miss
Aino Vare, in Brooklyn.

TRIP TO HELSINKI

THE DANCE

Finnish

Formation: For any number of couples in two parallel lines facing each other, about ten feet apart. Men in one line on the right from the front, women on the left. Hands are joined along each line. (See Diagram 1.)

Step: Running step.

First Figure

Diag. 1

Meas. 1-2: The two lines take six running steps forward toward each other beginning with the right foot. (See Diagram 1.)

Meas. 3-4: Lines move backward to place with six running steps beginning with the right foot.

Meas. 1-4 (repeated): As above.

Chorus

Diag. 2

Measures 5-8 are played through twice.

Meas. 5-6: All drop joined hands and stand motionless.

Meas. 7: All take one step sideward to the left with the left foot (*count "one"*). Pause (*count "two"*). Bring heels together (right to left foot; *count "three"*).

Meas. 8: Men bow and women curtsy (*counts "one—two—three"*). (See Diagram 2.)

Diag. 3

Meas. 5-6: All stand in place, motionless.

Meas. 7: Men make a quarter turn to the left stepping on the left foot, women to the right with the right foot (*count "one"*). Pause (*count "two"*). Bring heels together (*count "three"*).

Meas. 8: Face front (*counts "one — two — three"*). (See Diagram 3.)

The Trip

Meas. 1-8: First couple's arms are free. Every person back of the first man and woman places both hands on the shoulders of the person in front of him. With a running step the first couple cast off, with the man turning to the left and the woman to the right. (See Diagram 3.) They run to the bottom of the set, with lines following, and back to original positions.

Repeat music as many times as necessary.

Second Figure (Threading the needle)

Meas. 1-8: The lines face each other as at the beginning with hands joined.. The first man runs forward and back under the arch formed by the second and third man, taking the line with him. He does the figure moving down towards the end of the line. The women in the opposite line do the same. (See Diagram 4.)
Repeat music as many times as necessary.

Chorus and the Trip

Meas. 5-8 (play twice): Repeat Chorus.

Meas. 1-8: Repeat the Trip. On reaching original positions, partners join hands.

Diag. 4   Diag. 5

Third Figure (The waves)

Meas. 1-8: (play as many times as needed): Couple One face about (so as to face Couple Two); Couple Three face about (so as to face Couple Four); and so on down the line. The odd-numbered couples face the foot of the set and the even-numbered couples. The even-numbered couples face the head of the set, the music, and the odd-numbered couples. With a walking step, the two couples facing change places with each other, even-numbered couples going under the arch formed by the odd-numbered couples. Now Couples One, Three, and Five face Couples Four, Six, and Eight, respectively. They change places again in the same manner except that this time the odd-numbered couples pass under the arch formed by the even-numbered couples. (See Diagram 5.)

Continue in this way all the way down the set and back, making the arch and passing under alternately until all are back in their original positions. In the meantime each couple on reaching the head or foot of the set turns to face the set and make an arch to continue in the manner prescribed above, after waiting one turn.

Chorus and the Trip

Meas. 5-8 (*play twice*): Repeat Chorus.
Meas. 1-8: Repeat the Trip.

The man kneels for his lady in many a folk dance as she dances around him. About these Norwegian costumes, note that the man sports fancy, intricately designed stockings, whereas the woman modestly wears black cotton ones!

LANGUAGE

FRENCH For Beginners
FRENCH GRAMMAR (CO)
GERMAN For Beginners
GERMAN GRAMMAR (CO)
ITALIAN For Beginners
LATIN (introductory course) (CO)
SPANISH For Beginners
SPANISH GRAMMAR (CO)

LITERATURE

AMERICAN LITERATURE (CO)
ENGLISH LITERATURE,
　HANDBOOK of
ENGLISH LITERATURE to Dryden (CO)
ENGLISH LITERATURE since Milton (CO)
NOVELS, Plot Outlines of 100
WORLD LITERATURE, 2 vols. (CO)

MATHEMATICS, ENGINEERING

ALGEBRA, College (CO)
ALGEBRA PROBLEMS
CALCULUS (CO)
ENGINEERING DRAWING (CO)
GEOMETRY, Analytic (CO)
GEOMETRY, Analytic: Problems (CO)
GEOMETRY, College
GEOMETRY, Engineering Descriptive (CO)
GEOMETRY, Plane: Problems (CO)
LOGARITHMIC & Trigonometric
　Tables (CO)
MATHEMATICS For Everyday Use
MATHEMATICS, COLLEGE (CO)
SLIDE RULE
TRIGONOMETRY, Plane &
　Spherical (CO)

PHILOSOPHY, RELIGION

PHILOSOPHERS, IDEAS of the Great
PHILOSOPHY: An Introduction (CO)
PHILOSOPHY, Handbook in the
　History of (CO)
PHILOSOPHY, Readings in (CO)
RELIGIONS of the World

PSYCHOLOGY

PSYCHIATRY For the Layman
PSYCHOLOGISTS: Theories, Discoveries,
　& Experiments of Great
PSYCHOLOGY, ABNORMAL (CO)
PSYCHOLOGY, CHILD (CO)
PSYCHOLOGY, EDUCATIONAL (CO)
PSYCHOLOGY, GENERAL (CO)
PSYCHOLOGY, READINGS (CO)
TOWARD MATURITY

SCIENCE

ANATOMY and PHYSIOLOGY, 2 vols. (CO)
ANATOMY, Atlas of Human
BACTERIOLOGY (CO)
BIOLOGY (CO)
BOTANY (CO)
CHEMISTRY, First-Year College (CO)
CHEMISTRY, Organic (CO)
CHEMISTRY, Physical (CO)
CHEMISTRY PROBLEMS (CO)
FOOD and YOU
GEOLOGY (CO)
PHYSICS (CO)
PHYSICS, PROBLEMS in (CO)
PHYSICS Without Mathematics (CO)
PHYSIOLOGY, Fundamentals of
ROCKS and MINERALS
ZOOLOGY (CO)

SOCIOLOGY, ANTHROPOLOGY

ANTHROPOLOGY, GENERAL (CO)
MAN and SOCIETY
SEX and MARRIAGE
SOCIOLOGY, Principles of (CO)
SOCIOLOGY, Readings in (CO)

SOCIAL ACTIVITIES, SPORTS

BRIDGE, First Book of
BRIDGE PLAYERS' Guide to Bidding
BRIDGE: Play of the Hand
CHECKERS, How to Play
CHESS, ATTACK and Counterattack in
CHESS, First Book of
CHESS GAMES, How to Win Quickly
CHESS, Improving Your
CHESS: 1001 Sacrifices and Combinations
CHESS OPENINGS, Complete Book of
CLUB MEMBER'S Handbook
COIN COLLECTION: How to Build
DANCE, HOW TO
FISHING, SPIN
FISHING, Sportsman's Digest of
FOLK DANCES For All
HUNTING, Sportsman's Digest of
MANNERS FOR MILLIONS
PARTY GAMES For All

STUDY AIDS

EXAMINATIONS, How to Write Better (CO)
EXAMINATIONS in COLLEGE,
　How to Take (CO)
HANDWRITING, BETTER
RESEARCH and REPORT WRITING (CO)
STUDY, BEST METHODS of (CO)
WRITING TERM PAPERS
　and REPORTS (CO)